PHILIPPE LEGENDRE

# KIDS CAN DRAW

# Arctic Animals

Walter Foster Publishing, Inc.
23062 La Cadena Drive
Laguna Hills, CA 92653 USA
ISBN 1-56010-269-1

© 1994, Editions Fleurus, Paris.
Text on pages 4-24 © 1997, Walter Foster Publishing, Inc. All rights reserved.
Original title *J'apprends á dessiner les animaux du Grand Nord,* © 1994, Editions Fleurus, Paris.

## Attention Parents and Teachers

All children can draw a circle, a square, or a triangle…which means that they can also learn to draw a walrus, wolf, or moose! The KIDS CAN DRAW learning method is easy and fun. Children will learn a technique and a vocabulary of shapes that will form the basis for all kinds of drawing.

Pictures are created by combining geometric shapes to form a mass of volumes and surfaces. From this stage, children can give character to their sketches with straight, curved, or broken lines.

With just a few strokes of the pencil, an Arctic animal will appear—and with the addition of color, the picture will be real work of art!

The KIDS CAN DRAW method offers a real apprenticeship in technique and a first look at composition, proportion, shapes, and lines. The simplicity of this method ensures that the pleasure of drawing is always the most important factor.

## About Philippe Legendre

French painter, engraver, and illustrator, Philippe Legendre also runs a school of art for children aged 6–14 years. Legendre frequently spends time in schools and has developed this method of learning so that all children can discover the artist within themselves.

# Helpful Tips

1. Each picture is made up of simple geometric shapes, which are illustrated at the top of the left-hand page. This is called the **Vocabulary of Shapes.** Encourage children to practice drawing each shape before starting their pictures.

2. Suggest children use a pencil to do their sketches. This way, if they don't like a particular shape, they can just erase it and try again.

3. A dotted line indicates that the line should be erased. Have children draw the whole shape and then erase the dotted part of the line.

4. Once children finish their drawings, they can color them with crayons, colored pencils, or felt-tip markers. They may want to go over the lines with a black pencil or pen.

## Now let's get started!

Her sweet round face…

shows that maybe…

this little seal…

is just a baby.

# Baby Seal

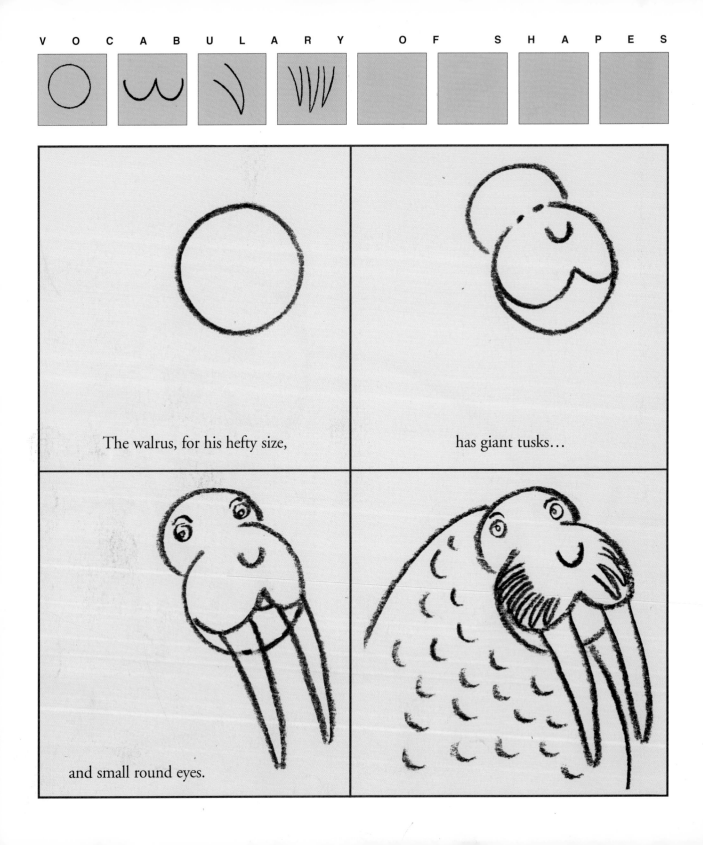

The walrus, for his hefty size,

has giant tusks…

and small round eyes.

# Walrus

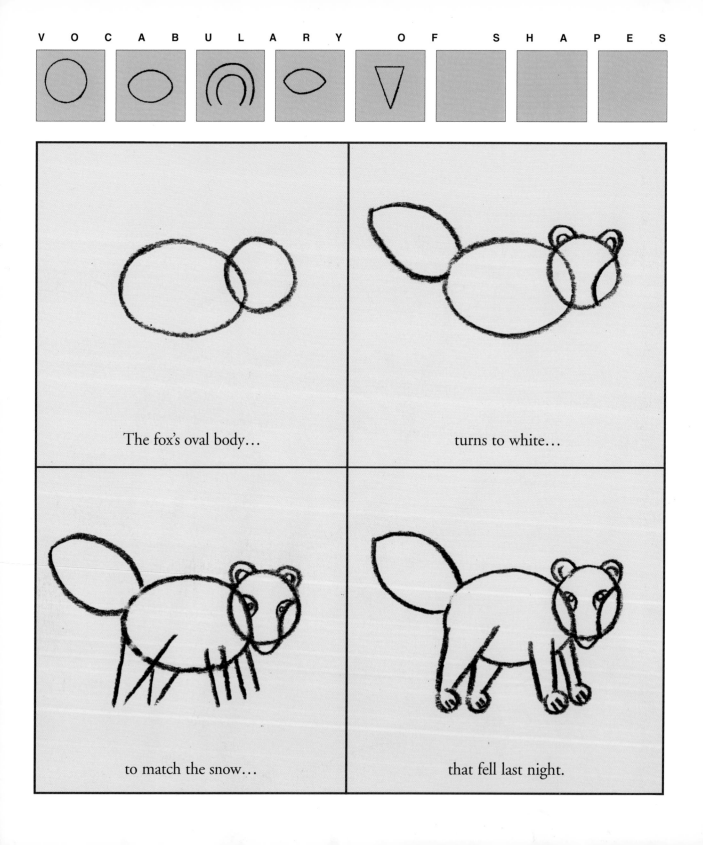

VOCABULARY OF SHAPES

The fox's oval body...

turns to white...

to match the snow...

that fell last night.

# Arctic Fox

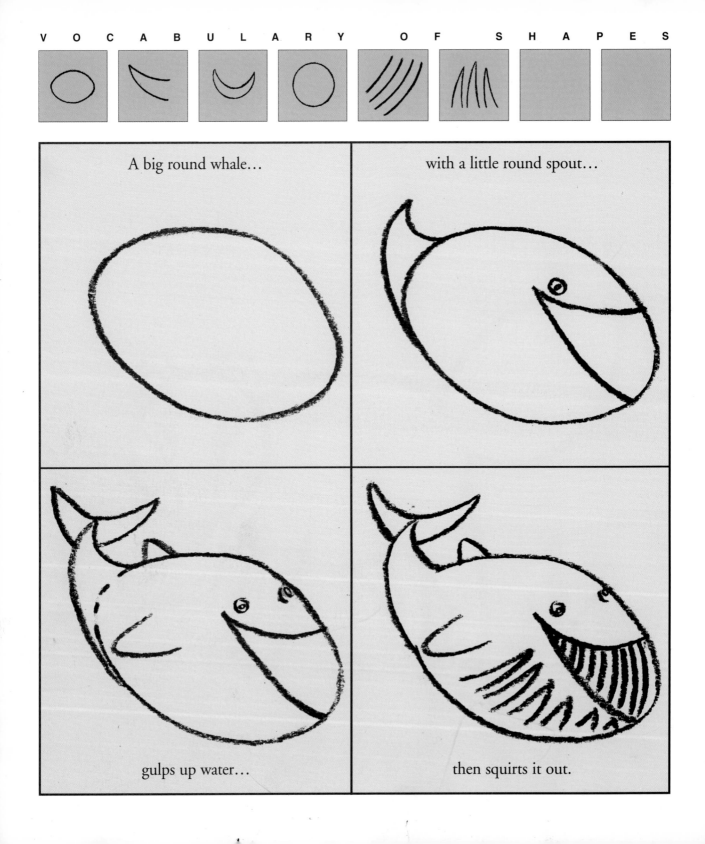

A big round whale…

with a little round spout…

gulps up water…

then squirts it out.

# **B**lue **W**hale

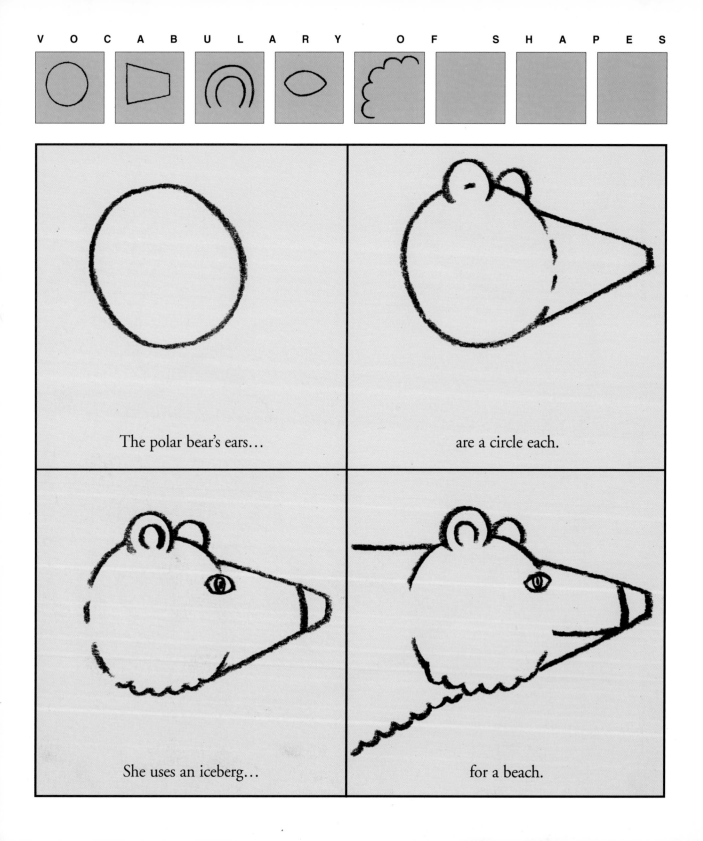

VOCABULARY OF SHAPES

The polar bear's ears…

are a circle each.

She uses an iceberg…

for a beach.

# **P**olar **B**ear

The musk ox has curving horns…

and a woolen coat…

to keep him warm.

# **M**usk **O**x

A triangle forms the wolf's snout.

Now draw some fur—

it's freezing out!

# **W**olf

His rounded antlers are called a "rack."

In fall they drop off;

in spring they grow back.

# **M**oose

VOCABULARY OF SHAPES

The puffin has a colorful beak…

plus red, webbed feet…

to walk across the snow and sleet.

# Puffin

The Arctic is a land so cold that water often freezes.

It's a wonder animals there don't get coughs and sneezes!

# Draw-along fun for children!

With the **"I Can Draw"** series, kids ages 6 and up will have hours of fun drawing amazing pictures of all the things they like best—animals, cartoons, creepy creatures, race cars, and more. Each book is full of colorful step-by-step illustrations with easy-to-follow instructions, explaining how to draw almost anything from basic shapes kids already know, such as circles, squares, triangles, and ovals. Each 40-page book includes 8 pages of grid paper.

# More step-by-step fun for young artists!

Our 6 **"I Can Draw"** Drawing Kits come with an instruction book and all the materials kids need for drawing their favorite subjects. Each kit includes colored pencils, sharpener, eraser, and grid paper pad. These handy kits make great gifts for home, school, or travel.

*Walter Foster*

**For a free catalog, write to: Walter Foster Publishing, Inc. 23062 La Cadena Drive, Laguna Hills, CA 92653. Or call (800) 426-0099.**